GATEWAYS AND PORTALS FOR LAW

These sites provide ways into legal resources on the web

AustLII — www.austlii.edu.au
Australian Legal Information Institute links to World Law as well as Australian material

BAILII — www.bailii.org
British & Irish Legal Information Institute. Under development

CataLaw — www.catalaw.com
Legal meta-index with a flexible search interface and very broad coverage

Cornell LII — www.law.cornell.edu
Cornell Legal Information Institute. Predominantly American, but contains worldwide links

Findlaw — www.findlaw.com/index.html
Extensive site with links to worldwide legal information

GLIN — lcweb2.loc.gov/law/GLINv1
The Global Legal Information Network at the Library of Congress

Hieros Gamos — www.hg.org
Major site, with worldwide information and versions in German, French, Italian and Spanish

JURIST — jurist.law.pitt.edu
Legal education network with links to an extensive body of materials for the academic community

JURIST UK — www.law.cam.ac.uk/jurist/index.htm
JURIST site with UK orientated material. Other JURIST sites exist for Canada and Australia

Jurweb
www.uni-bayreuth.de/students/jurweb
Legal Information on the Internet. Useful site from the University of Bayreuth

LAWLINKS
www.ukc.ac.uk/library/lawlinks
Sarah Carter's site at the University of Kent

Portal to Legal Resources in the UK and Ireland
www.venables.co.uk
The most comprehensive site for practitioner orientated legal information in the UK

SOSIG Law
www.sosig.ac.uk/law
Links to quality internet resources with detailed descriptions of their contents

UK LEGISLATION

These sites will lead you to the legislative information on the web for the UK. For details of the legislation of Scotland, Wales and Northern Ireland see under Devolved Governments below p 11

Gateways

BAILII
www.bailii.org
The British and Irish Legal Information Institute has a pilot site which will cover all UK and Irish legislation and case law, fully hyperlinked. Under development, but already a useful starting point

LAWLINKS
www.ukc.ac.uk/library/lawlinks/resources.htm
Sarah Carter's website at the University of Kent

UKState.com
www.ukstate.com
The Stationery Office's new gateway to official information contains links to UK legislation including Scottish, Welsh and Northern Irish legislation from 1987. Look under Your Government. Site under development

United Kingdom Legislation www.legislation.hmso.gov.uk
Links to all the sites for UK legislation listed below

Primary and secondary legislation

Acts of Parliament www.hmso.gov.uk/acts.htm
From 1996 all Public Acts have been published in full text, and Local Acts since 1997. There are summaries of a range of earlier Acts

Explanatory Notes www.legislation.hmso.gov.uk/legislation/uk-expa.htm
Explanatory notes to Public Acts introduced into Parliament by a government minister are available from 1999. These give very useful background

Chronological and Alphabetical lists of Acts www.infolaw.co.uk
These consolidated lists of all Acts in full text and summary are provided on the Infolaw site

Statutory Instruments www.hmso.gov.uk
From 1997 in full text, usually appearing within 14 days. The site also includes draft SIs

Progress of legislation

Bills before Parliament www.parliament.the-stationery-office.co.uk/pa/pabills.htm
These include Explanatory notes for Bills introduced into Parliament by Government ministers. Amendments are added as they are published.

Weekly Information Bulletin www.parliament.the-stationery-office.co.uk/pa/cm/cmwib.htm
Contains recent and forthcoming business of the House of Commons. Includes a full list of Bills introduced in the current session, with details of their progress through Parliament

House of Commons Hansard www.publications.parliament.uk/pa/cm/cmpubns.htm
Includes daily debates back to session 1988/89, and Standing Committee debates on Bills from 1997/98

UK CASE LAW

Gateways

BAILII
Pilot site which at present provides a searchable database of all UK case law currently available on the web. The cases have their own system of citation.

www.bailii.org

Westlaw UK
All UK legislation in force with commentary

www.westlaw.co.uk

Lexis
Statutes and Statutory Instruments in force

www.lexis-nexis.com

Lawtel
Full text of Acts since 1990 (unamended). Access to commencements and repeals. Links to SIs

www.lawtel.co.uk

Justis Statutes and Justis Statutory Instruments
All Acts as enacted with links to amending and amended legislation. Statutory Instruments from 1987

www.justis.com

Butterworths Legislation Direct
Contains all UK legislation in force with the ability to view historical versions

www.butterworths.co.uk

Subscription services containing full text legislation
See Subscription Services below p 72 for details of these

House of Lords Hansard
Debates back to June 1996

www.publications.parliament.uk/pa/ld/ldhansrd.htm

LAWLINKS www.ukc.ac.uk/library/lawlinks/resources.htm
Sarah Carter's website at the University of Kent

Transcripts of cases

House of Lords Judgments www.parliament.the-stationery-office.co.uk/pa/ld/ldjudinf.htm
On the web from 1996, they are available 2 hours after the judgment is handed down. To search for a particular case use BAILII above rather than the search engine on this site

Court of Appeal and High Court www.courtservice.gov.uk
Selected judgments are available on the Court Service website, via a searchable database. New cases are listed at the top level

Employment Appeal Tribunal www.employmentappeals.gov.uk
All EAT judgments from 2000

Social Security and Child Support Commissioners www.hywels.demon.co.uk/commrs/decns.htm
Selected decisions from 1991 are available on this site, and also via the Court Service (see above)

Times Law Reports www.the-times.co.uk
The newspaper is available online from 1996. To find a law report you need to know the date, and go to the Back Issues

Indexes to case law

The major indexes to case law are available as subscription services only. See below

Daily Law Notes www.lawreports.co.uk/indexdln.htm
Daily summaries of significant decisions of the House of Lords, the Privy Council, the Court of Appeal, all divisions of the High Court and the European Court of Justice, prepared by the Incorporated Council of Law Reporting

Swarbrick & Co: Law Index www.swarb.co.uk
An index to cases from 1992, arranged by date, legislation, area of law and court

Subscription services containing case law

See Subscription Services below p 72 for details of these

Butterworths All England Direct   www.butterworths.co.uk
The All England Law Reports, together with the All England Reporter, a digest of new cases and next day access to handed down judgments and transcripts of cases

Current Legal Information   www.smlawpub.co.uk
Contains the Case Citator, an index of cases from 1947 with judicial history, citations, and links to a digest and case commentaries

Casetrack   www.casetrack.com
Transcripts of cases from the Court of Appeal, High Court, provided by court transcript agents Smith Bernal, from 1996

Justis   www.justis.com
Their collection of online databases include Electronic Law Reports, Weekly Law Reports, Lloyd's Reports, Criminal Appeal Reports, Industrial Cases Reports and many others

Lawtel   www.lawtel.co.uk
Summaries of cases back to 1980 with some earlier cases, with hyperlinks between cases and to legislation where available on the database

Lexis   www.lexis-nexis.com
Reports and transcripts of a comprehensive range of cases from 1945

New Law Online   www.cchnewlaw.co.uk
Digest of cases from 1995 with access to the handed down judgment where available and approved transcripts

Westlaw UK   www.westlaw.co.uk
Includes The Law Reports, Lloyd's Reports and a number of other series back to 1947

INDEXES TO JOURNAL ARTICLES

See Subscription Services below p 72 for details of these. See also Electronic Legal Journals under Legal Publishing below p 70

Index to Legal Periodicals   hwwilsonweb.com
Indexes American and UK academic journals from 1981

Lawtel   www.lawtel.co.uk
Indexes around 50 UK journals from 1998

Legal Journals Index   www.smlawpub.co.uk or westlaw.co.uk
This indexes over 400 UK and European English language journals from 1986, and is available on Current Legal Information (CD-ROM and online) and Westlaw

CURRENT AWARENESS AND NEWS OF LEGAL AFFAIRS

Legal sites

Butterworths   www.butterworths.co.uk
This has a site called News Direct giving daily legal news updates

The Gazette   www.lawgazette.co.uk
Online edition of the Law Society Gazette, with an archive of earlier issues

Interactive Lawyer   www.interactive-lawyer.com
Online community offering daily legal news

The Lawyer   www.the-lawyer.co.uk
The current edition of the journal

New Law Journal   www.butterworths.co.uk/nlj
The current edition of the journal

Sweet & Maxwell   www.smlawpub.co.uk:
This website includes a What's New alerting service, and a number of online services including the BADGER Alerter (current awareness for law), the European Alerter and European Union News

NEWS MEDIA

BBC   www.news.bbc.co.uk
ITN   www.itn.co.uk
The Financial Times   www.ft.com
The Guardian   www.guardian.co.uk
The Independent   www.independent.co.uk
The Telegraph   www.telegraph.co.uk
The Times   www.the-times.co.uk
AJR Newslink   ajr.newslink.org/news.html
Links to newspapers and other media across the world

News information for education   www.niss.ac.uk/news/index.html
Provides links to newspapers worldwide

STUDENT RESOURCES

Butterworths Academic   www.butterworths.co.uk/academic/index.htm
Resources for students, including Case Notes, an overview of recent case law

Cavendish Publishing   www.cavendishpublishing.com/lawstu/index.asp
The Studentzone includes news, new cases and the Student Law Review back issues

Consilio   www.spr-consilio.com
Interactive online magazine for law students. Includes articles and LLB/CPE revision materials, featuring a different area of law each month

Law Careers Net   www.lawcareers.net
The Trainee Solicitors Group site provides careers information for would be lawyers

Law Student   www.lawstudent.co.uk
Site developed by law students for law students

Mooting Net   www.mootingnet.org.uk
Materials for mooting

Student Law Centre   www.studentlaw.com
Site from Legalease with extensive information on practice, pupillages, training vacancies and placements

Student News & Case Summaries   www.lawreports.co.uk/indexn4.htm
The Incorporated Council of Law Reporting provides a student site with case summaries and articles

UK Law Online   www.leeds.ac.uk/law/hamlyn
A site which contains a description of the UK legal systems, with extensive links. Not updated since 1998

DEVOLVED GOVERNMENTS

SCOTLAND

Official legal sites

Scottish Legislation   www.scotland-legislation.hmso.gov.uk
This official government site links to Acts of the Scottish Parliament from 1999, Explanatory Notes to the Acts and Scottish Statutory Instruments, as well as UK legislation applying to Scotland

Scottish Courts website   **www.scotcourts.gov.uk**
Judgments of the Court of Session, the High Court of Justiciary, the Sheriff Courts, as well as other information on the Scottish court system

Scottish Parliament   **www.scottish.parliament.uk**
This site links to information on the Scottish parliament, including reports of proceedings

Scottish Executive   **www.scotland.gov.uk**
The Scottish civil service website

BAILII   **www.bailii.org**
British and Irish Legal Information Institute pilot site includes links to Scottish cases and legislation. This site is under development, and will be fully hyperlinked

Secondary material

Guide to Scots Law   **www.gla.ac.uk/Clubs/WebSoc/~9506878a/guide/guide.html**
Student produced guide presented in Q & A format from Glasgow University School of Law

Law Society of Scotland   **www.lawscot.org.uk**
Includes 'What is Scots Law?' a description of the court structure, history and origins of Scots law

Scots Law News   **www.law.ed.ac.uk/sln**
Legal news provided by the Editor of the Edinburgh Law Review

Scots Law Times   **www.wgreen.co.uk/slt**
Index to the journal with catchwords for new cases

The Scotsman   **www.scotsman.com**
Online edition of the newspaper

WALES

Wales Legislation www.wales-legislation.hmso.gov.uk
Links to Welsh Statutory Instruments and to Acts of the UK Parliament applying to Wales

National Assembly for Wales www.wales.gov.uk
Information on the Welsh Assembly, including the record of proceedings

NORTHERN IRELAND

Northern Ireland Legislation www.northernireland-legislation.hmso.gov.uk
This includes Acts of the N Ireland Assembly with Explanatory Notes, Statutory Rules of N Ireland from 1998, links to NI Orders in Council from 1997, the N Ireland Act 1998 and associated delegated legislation, and links to UK Acts applying to N Ireland

Northern Ireland Assembly www.ni-assembly.gov.uk
Information about the Assembly including the official report and video coverage from the Assembly Chamber (when not suspended)

IRELAND

BAILII www.bailii.org
British & Irish Legal Information Institute offers free access to Irish legislation and case law

CAIN cain.ulst.ac.uk
Conflict Archive on the Internet: Extensive information and source material on the Northern Ireland conflict

Irish Law Site www.ucc.ie/ucc/depts/law/irishlaw
Compiled at University College, Cork, this site has excellent links, including to referenda and the peace process

Irish Government   **www.irlgov.ie**
Includes debates and other material from the Houses of the Oireachtas (Parliament) and links to other government sites

The Law Society of Ireland   **www.lawsociety.ie**
An excellent entry point for research on Irish law

Office of the Attorney General   **www.irlgov.ie/ag**
This site includes a database of Irish legislation: Acts of the Oireachtas 1922–97

UK GOVERNMENT

Gateways

Government Information Service   **www.open.gov.uk**
The starting point for government information, you can find information on this site by organisation and topic. Valuable 'What's New' page for keeping up to date. The A-Z index of all government departments, agencies, local authorities, etc, is a mine of information. There is also an arrangement by topic

Inforoute   **www.hmso.gov.uk/inforoute**
A search engine and central information point for official government information and materials

Direct Access Government   **www.dag-business.gov.uk**
The government's small business service, including regulatory guidance and forms on government websites

Gateway to official legal services

Lord Chancellor's Department   **www.open.gov.uk/lcd**
Excellent site, containing a wealth of information on the administration of justice. One of the best places to start for legal information and as a gateway to other legal sites. Also contains the Civil Procedure Rules

Legal departments and agencies

A selection – see the LCD (above) for more links and the Government Information Service for a comprehensive listing

Cabinet Office   **www.cabinet-office.gov.uk**
Information on the government machine, including ministries, the civil service, government issues

Community Legal Service   **www.justask.org.uk**
Creates a network of organisations offering legal and advice services to the public

Crown Prosecution Service   **www.cps.gov.uk**
The government department which prosecutes people charged with a criminal offence

Law Commission   **www.lawcom.gov.uk**
The site includes information on the Law Commission's project, 'Law Under Review' – the law reform bulletin, and under 'Library' the full text of recent Law Commission consultation papers and reports

Legal Services Commission   **www.legalservices.gov.uk**
Public body created under the Access to Justice Act 1999 to administer the Community Legal Service and the Criminal Defence Service

Parliamentary Ombudsman   **www.ombudsman.org.uk**
Information on putting complaints to the Parliamentary Ombudsman, and the Scottish, Welsh and Health Service ombudsmen

A selection of other government departments

Department for Education and Employment	www.dfee.gov.uk
Department of the Environment, Transport and the Regions	www.detr.gov.uk
Department of Health	www.doh.gov.uk
Department of Social Security	www.dss.gov.uk

Department of Trade and Industry	www.dti.gov.uk
Home Office	www.homeoffice.gov.uk
Office of National Statistics	www.ons.gov.uk

OFFICIAL PUBLICATIONS

Indexes and other sources

NB: Departmental or agency websites are often the best place to find their own publications

BOPCAS   www.soton.ac.uk/~bopcas

A subscription service which contains a free browsable monthly index for the past six months for official publications

Daily List   www.the-stationery-office.co.uk/daily_list

The Daily List provides bibliographic details of government publications. You have to know the date of publication to use it retrospectively, as it is not searchable

Official Documents site   www.official-documents.co.uk

Flags the most important new document of the day, and links to UK publications, in which you can find documents arranged by date, title, department and category

The Stationery Office   www.the-stationery-office.co.uk

Website for the major publisher of government publications Amongst other resources it links to UKState which includes a Bookstore for tracing and ordering official publications

What's New   www.open.gov.uk/cctagis/whatsnew.htm

The What's New page on the Government Information Service site includes links to new web based publications from departments or agencies

Subscription services for official publications

See Subscription Services below p 72 for details of these

Current Legal Information   www.smlawpub.co.uk
Contains the BADGER database for 'grey literature' – reports and official or semi-official publications from all sources

Lawtel   www.lawtel.co.uk
Contains links to new official publications and parliamentary information

UKOP   www.ukop.co.uk
United Kingdom Official Publications. A comprehensive searchable database

PARLIAMENT

UK Parliament   www.parliament.uk
The official website for the Houses of Parliament

House of Commons   www.parliament.uk/commons/hsecom.htm
All the business of the House of Commons – general information, Committees, debates, and publications including the useful House of Commons Research Papers

House of Commons Publications   www.publications.parliament.uk/pa/cm/cmpubns.htm
These contain a mass of information, including the House of Commons Weekly Information Bulletin, for current proceedings, Standing Committee debates, Select Committee publications and much else

House of Lords   www.parliament.the-stationery-office.co.uk/pa/ld/ldhome.htm
All the business of the House of Lords, including Committees, reports, judgments, debates

Hansard – House of Commons www.parliament.the-stationery-office.co.uk/pa/cm/cmhansrd.htm
Parliamentary debates, with an archive back to 1988/89

Hansard – House of Lords www.publications.parliament.uk/pa/ld/ldhansrd.htm
Full text debates back to 1996

SPECIAL LEGAL TOPICS

The emphasis is UK and European, but also includes some materials in international law

Gateways

AustLII www.austlii.edu.au/links/272.html
The Australian Legal Information Institute's World Law has a subject index

Findlaw www.findlaw.com/01topics/index.html
Resources listed under Legal Subjects. Mainly American, but useful for international material

Hieros Gamos www.hg.org/practiceareas.html
200 Practice Areas are identified on this site. American emphasis, but useful for international topics

LAWLINKS www.ukc.ac.uk/library/lawlinks/special.htm
Sarah Carter's site at the University of Kent has a listing by Special Legal Topics

Legal Scholarship on the World Wide Web www.law.cam.ac.uk/essays/schol.htm
An index to full text essays arranged by subject, from Cambridge University Law Faculty

Portal to Legal Resources in the UK and Ireland www.venables.co.uk
Delia Venables' site has a useful list of information sources by general subject area

ADMINISTRATION OF JUSTICE

Starting point

Lord Chancellor's Department www.open.gov.uk/lcd/lcdhome.htm
The definitive site, includes links to all relevant materials on access to justice, legal aid, the court service, the judiciary, community legal service, individual and family matters and much more

Other materials

Judicial Studies Board www.cix.co.uk/~jsb/index.htm
Training and instruction for judges in the UK. The site includes training materials

Lawrights www.lawrights.co.uk
Free legal advice service for people needing to take legal action themselves, with a wealth of information on the system

Lord Woolf's Inquiry on Civil Justice www.law.warwick.ac.uk/Woolf
All the materials gathered together on one site

Magistrates Association www.magistrates-association.org.uk
Informative page designed for the public as well as for magistrates themselves

National Association of Citizens Advice Bureaux www.nacab.org.uk
Legal and other advice for the public

Woolf Bytes www.woolf.co.uk/bytes.html
The College of Law's site, which includes free information as well as a subscription service

ANCIENT LAW

Roman Law www.jura.uni-sb.de/Rechtsgeschichte/Ius.Romanum/english.html
Discussion, links and texts in Roman law from Saarbrücken University. The site includes a Latin version

Roman Law Resources   www.abdn.ac.uk/~law113/rl/rl.htm
The Civil Law Centre, University of Aberdeen, hosts this site, which includes links to other Roman law resources

Online journal

Forum historiae iuris   www.rewi.hu-berlin.de/FHI

ARBITRATION

American Arbitration Association   www.adr.org
Dispute resolution services worldwide. The site includes articles from the Dispute Resolution Journal and other publications

ICSID   www.worldbank.org/icsid
International Centre for the Settlement of Investment Disputes. The site includes documents, publications and cases

International ADR   www.internationaladr.com
Information on international mediation and arbitration, including treaties, national arbitration laws, judicial decisions and arbitral awards, model clauses

International Commercial Arbitration   www.lib.uchicago.edu/~llou/intlarb.html
Comprehensive page of links to resources in print and electronic format from the D'Angelo Law Library, University of Chicago

Society of Maritime Arbitrators   www.smany.org
To foster ADR in maritime and related industries

BUSINESS AND FINANCE LAW

See also Electronic Commerce, International Commercial Law

Starting points

Biz/Ed   www.bized.ac.uk
An academic site containing a comprehensive internet catalogue of resources in business and learning materials for various levels of business courses

20

Business Information Resources on the Internet www.dis.strath.ac.uk/business/index.html
Long established website maintained by Sheila Webber at the University of Strathclyde

World Bank Law Library www1.worldbank.org/legal/lawlibrary.html
Good source for international materials and links to resources

Other materials

Banking Ombudsman www.obo.org.uk
Body for bankers in the UK. Information on the service, how to make a complaint, summary of the annual report

CAROL www.carol.co.uk
Company Annual Reports On Line: a free service covering Europe (including UK), Asia and USA

Competition Online www.clubi.ie/competition/compframesite/index.htm
Includes a 'the world's biggest competition, anti-trust and regulatory sites list', plus news, articles and other information

Financial Times www.ft.com
A wealth of up to date information on the newspaper website

International Centre for Commercial Law www.icclaw.com
Legalease's site includes articles containing information on new legislation, developments and cases in specialist practice areas of commercial law

JOLIS jolis.worldbankimflib.org/external.htm
Joint Bank-Fund Library Network, consisting of 14 libraries working together to provide information to World Bank and IMF staff

LawMoney www.lawmoney.com
Site for the legal profession with an international focus

Mondaq Business Briefing www.businessmonitor.co.uk
Up to date articles and briefings on business matters

Money Laundering and Compliance Website　　　　www.countermoneylaundering.com
The detection and prevention of fraud, including many resources and links

UK Bankruptcy and Insolvency Website　　　　www.insolvency.co.uk
Site aimed at legal practitioners, with detailed information

Organisations

Bank for International Settlements　　　　www.bis.org
British Bankers' Association　　　　www.bba.co.uk
Financial Services Authority　　　　www.fsa.gov.uk
International Business Law Consortium　　　　www.iblc.com
World Bank　　　　www.worldbank.org

Online journals

Stanford Journal of Law, Business & Finance　　　　www.stanford.edu/group/sjlbf
Trusts & Trustees　　　　www.trusts-and-trustees.com

COMPUTER LAW

See also Business and Finance, Electronic Commerce, Intellectual Property

Data Protection Registrar　　　　www.dataprotection.gov.uk
The website includes reports and specialist papers as well as the new law

Hieros Gamos Computers and the Law　　　　www.hg.org/compute.html
Comprehensive starting point for research

Information Society Directorate General　　www.ispo.cec.be/infosoc/telecompolicy/Welcome.htm
The Communications policy page includes access to the text of all EU legislation since 1996, and a selection of earlier documents from 1984

Information Society Website   www.ispo.cec.be
The European Union's Information Society Promotion Office for access to material on EU policy

Masons Computer Law Reports   www.masons.com/library/reports
Full text cases relating to the computer and telecommunications industries

Organisations

Computer Law Association (US)   www.cla.org
Society for Computers and Law (UK)   www.scl.org

Online journals

Berkeley Technology Law Journal	www.law.berkeley.edu/journals/btlj
Computer Law Review and Technology Journal (Southern Methodist U)	www.smu.edu/~csr/smuscr.htm
Cyberspace Law Journal	raven.cc.ukans.edu/~cybermom/CLJ/clj.html
Droit de l'Informatique et des Télécoms	www.dit.presse.fr
IDEA – Journal of Law and Technology	www.idea.fplc.edu
International Journal of Communications Law and Policy	www.digital-law.net/IJCLP
JILT: Journal of Information Law and Technology	elj.warwick.ac.uk/jilt
Journal of Online Law (College of William and Mary School of Law)	www.wm.edu/law/publications/jol
Journal of Science and Technology Law (Boston University)	www.bu.edu/law/scitech
Michigan Telecommunications and Technology Law Journal	www.mttlr.org
Revista Electrónica de Derecho Informático	publicaciones.derecho.org/redi
Richmond Journal of Law and Technology	www.urich.edu/~jolt
Stanford Technology Law Review	stlr.stanford.edu/STLR
Virginia Journal of Law and Technology	www.vjolt.net
West Virginia Journal of Law and Technology	www.wvjolt.wvu.edu/indexhome.htm

CONSTITUTIONAL LAW

Includes material on the UK Human Rights Act and the incorporation of the European Convention on Human Rights into UK law. See also Human Rights p 60

Starting points

Lord Chancellor's Department: Human Rights   www.open.gov.uk/lcd/humanrights/humanrfr.htm
Excellent starting point with information on the Human Rights Bill and Act, the Lord Chancellor's communications to the judiciary, press notices, speeches, comparative links, and a reading list

Researching Constitutional Law on the Internet   www.lib.uchicago.edu/~llou/conlaw.html
Invaluable research guide containing material from all over the world, in spite of starting from a US base. University of Chicago D'Angelo Law Library

Echr.Net   www.echr.net
Aims to provide a comprehensive source of information on human rights for lawyers, including recent case law, comparative judgments from other countries and much else

Other materials

Constitution Finder   www.urich.edu/~jpjones/confinder
An index to constitutions throughout the world

Constitution Unit   www.ucl.ac.uk/constitution-unit
Independent research body on constitutional change, at University College London's School of Public Policy. The site includes a Monitor of current issues, briefings and reports of research

International Constitutional Law   www.uni-wuerzburg.de/law/home.html
Links to constitutions of all countries

Interparliamentary Union   www.ipu.org
Information on national parliaments across the world. Includes a database of bibliographic references

Civil rights organisations

Campaign for Freedom of Information	www.cfoi.org.uk
Charter 88	www.charter88.org.uk
Commission for Racial Equality	www.cre.gov.uk
Children's Legal Centre	www2.essex.ac.uk/clc
Equal Opportunities Commission	www.eoc.org.uk
Joint Council for the Welfare of Immigrants	www.jcwi.org.uk
Legal Action Group	www.lag.org.uk
Liberty	www.liberty-human-rights.org.uk
Statewatch	www.statewatch.org

Online journals

Law and Contemporary Problems (Duke University)	www.law.duke.edu/journals/lcp
University of Pennsylvania Journal of Constitutional Law	www.law.upenn.edu/conlaw

CONTRACT LAW

Advertising Law Resource Center   www.lawpublish.com
Mainly American, aimed at the advertising industry but including many resources of more general interest

Center for Research on Contracts and the Structure of Enterprise   crcse.business.pitt.edu
Site launched at the University of Pittsburg, includes a Digital Contracts Database and Working Papers

CLAB Europa   europa.eu.int/clab
European database of case law on unfair contractual terms from the EU Health and Consumer Protection Directorate General

Consumer Law   www.fs.dk/uk/acts/eu/0-eu.htm
Selected EU material from the Danish Consumer Council, including directives and judgments

Department of Trade and Industry   www.dti.gov.uk
All the material covered by the DTI, including links to agencies such as the Consumer Affairs Directorate

Health and Consumer Protection Directorate General europa.eu.int/comm/dgs/health_consumer/index_en.htm
Website of the European Union's DG

Office of Fair Trading   www.oft.gov.uk
The government department's website

Principles of European Contract Law   www.jus.uio.no/lm/eu.contract.principles.1998/doc.html
Complete revised version by the Commission on European Contract Law, published 1988

Restitution and Unjust Enrichment   www.law.cam.ac.uk/restitution/restitution.htm
Course materials, including articles, bibliographies, case law and a discussion list. Steve Hedley at Cambridge University

Trading Standards Net   www.tradingstandards.net
Trading standards and consumer related advice and information

CRIMINAL JUSTICE

Starting points

Penal Lexicon   www.penlex.org.uk
Everything you need on prisons, penal affairs and the criminal justice system, mainly UK, but some worldwide resources. A valuable source for full text documents

Police Law   www.policelaw.co.uk
Informative site covering all aspects of criminal justice in the UK with links beyond, with particular emphasis on policing issues.

UK Criminal Justice Web Links   www.leeds.ac.uk/law/ccjs/ukweb.htm
The Centre for Criminal Justice at Leeds University provides a good starting point. The site includes sections on Continental Europe, North America and the rest of the world

Other materials

Australian Institute of Criminology   www.aic.gov.au
Includes articles and research publications in full text as well as extensive information on the criminal justice system in Australia

Criminal Justice System Website   www.criminal-justice-system.gov.uk
Gathers together all the agencies responsible for criminal justice in England and Wales

Federal Justice Statistics Resource Centre   fjsrc.urban.org
Information about suspects and defendants in the US criminal justice system

Home Office   www.homeoffice.gov.uk
Information on all the matters covered by the Home Office, with details of current programmes

Home Office Research Development and Statistics Directorate   www.homeoffice.gov.uk/rds
Statistical information on all aspects of criminal justice, details of the RDS's research programme and links to full text publications

Howard League for Penal Reform   web.ukonline.co.uk/howard.league
Old established campaigning organisation

Lord Chancellor's Department: Criminal Matters   www.open.gov.uk/lcd/criminal/crimfr.htm
Gathers together official sources for the administration of criminal justice

UNICRI   www.unicri.it
United Nations Interregional Crime and Justice Research Institute, with information on its databases, projects, publications and documentation

World Factbook of Criminal Justice Systems   www.ojp.usdoj.gov/bjs/abstract/wfcj.htm
Site hosted by the US Bureau of Statistics

ELECTRONIC COMMERCE

See also Business and Finance law, International Commercial Law

Department of Trade and Industry   www.dti.gov.uk/CII/electronic.html
Extensive information provided by the DTI

Electronic Commerce and the European Union   www.ispo.cec.be/ecommerce
The EU Information Society Promotion Office (ISPO) website

Findlaw   cyber.findlaw.com/commerce
Comprehensive source for e-commerce documents

Global E-Commerce Law   www.bakerinfo.com/ecommerce
Baker & McKenzie's site containing legislation and regulations on e-commerce in jurisdictions worldwide as well as other materials including articles

Internet Law & Policy Forum   www.ilpf.org
International organisation dedicated to promoting global growth of e-commerce

Lex Mercatoria   www.jus.uio.no/lm/toc/x.00-electronic.commerce.html
E-commerce pages on this comprehensive site, with extensive links to documents and websites

United States Government   www.ecommerce.gov
US government's electronic commerce policy website

EMPLOYMENT LAW

British Employment Law   www.emplaw.co.uk
Site aimed at anyone requiring information on employment law

EIROnline   www.eiro.eurofound.ie
European Industrial Relations Observatory provides information and analysis on industrial relations in the EU

Employment Appeal Tribunal   www.employmentappeals.gov.uk
This site includes transcripts of recent EAT judgments, indexed by type of case

Federation of European Employers   www.euen co.uk
A site with a subscription service but also an excellent collection of primary texts in employment law

ILO   www.ilo.org
International Labour Organisation website. This includes access to ILOLEX, a database on ILO standards, and NATLEX, a database of national laws on labour, social security and related rights

Incomes Data Services   www.incomesdata co.uk
Up to date information on a wide range of employment law issues

Trades Union Congress   www.tuc.org.uk
The TUC website includes useful links to research and briefings on employment law issues

Online journal

Thompsons Labour and European Law Review   www.thompsons.law.co.uk/ltext/libindex.htm

ENVIRONMENTAL LAW

Starting points

DETR   www.detr.gov.uk
Department of Transport, Environment and the Regions website

ENDS   www.ends.co.uk/links
Environmental Data Services. This site includes a comprehensive list of links to sources on the environment

European Environmental Law
University of Maastricht. An excellent site

www.asser.nl/eel

Hieros Gamos World Environmental Law
Guide to worldwide resources

www.hg.org/environ.html

Other materials

ASIL Wildlife Interest Group
The American Society of International Law group's pages contain resources and links, including occasional papers

www.eelink.net/~asilwildlife

ELDIS
This site at the Institute of Development Studies, Sussex University, is a gateway to development information and includes much material on environmental affairs

www.ids.ac.uk/eldis

ENTRI
Environmental Treaties and Resource Indicators searchable database

sedac.ciesin.org/entri

Environment Directorate General
Comprehensive information on EU policy

europa.eu.int/comm/environment/index_en.htm

Globelaw
Contains material on international environmental law, including treaties and conventions

www.globelaw.com

The Green Channel
Environmental network, including interactive forums on environmental topics

www.greenchannel.com

GreenNet
Global computer network for environment, peace, human rights and development groups

www.gn.apc.org

Information for Industry
Information for environment professionals

www.ifi.co.uk

The Interactive Footpath — sh.plym.ac.uk/footpath
Legal policy and management issues related to public rights of way and access to the countryside in England and Wales, from Plymouth University

International Water Law Project — home.att.net/~intlh2olaw
American based site includes links to treaties and regional agreements, case law, a bibliography and internet resources on water law

World Conservation Monitoring Unit — www.wcmc.org.uk
Provides information services on conservation and sustainable development

Organisations

English Nature	www.english-nature.org.uk
Environment Agency	www.environment-agency.gov.uk
European Environment Agency	www.eea.eu.int
Friends of the Earth	www.foe.co.uk
Greenpeace	www.greenpeace.org
International Court of Environment Conciliation and Arbitration	www.greenchannel.com/iceac
IUCN: World Conservation Union	www.iucn.org
UKELA: United Kingdom Environmental Law Association	www.greenchannel.com/ukela
UNEP: United Nations Environment Programme	www.unep.org
WWF: World Wildlife Fund	www.wwf.org
WWF-UK: World Wildlife Fund, UK	www.wwf-uk.org
World Bank	www.worldbank.org

Online journals

CEPLMP On-Line Journal — www.dundee.ac.uk/cepmlp/journal
Duke Environmental Law & Policy Forum — www.law.duke.edu/journals/delpf
Electronic Green Journal — egj.lib.uidaho.edu
Journal of International Wildlife Law and Policy — www.jiwlp.com

FAMILY LAW

Starting point

Lord Chancellor's Department — www.open.gov.uk/lcd/family/famfr.htm
Individual and Family Matters on the LCD site. Links to all the official sources

Other materials

Carelaw — www.nchafc.org.uk/carelaw
A website giving information for young people in care in England and Wales

Child Welfare — www.childwelfare.com
American based organisation with worldwide links

Children's Legal Centre — www2.essex.ac.uk/clc
Charity concerned with law and policy affecting children and young people

Family Law Consortium — www.tflc.co.uk
This family law practice website has links to family welfare organisations

Jordans Family Law — www.familylaw.co.uk
The site includes access to a weekly update of new cases, legislation and practice directions

Pearl Willis Law Site — www.zyworld.com/familylaw
Barrister's website with excellent materials on family law

Social Security and Child Support Commissioners — www.hywels.demon.co.uk/commrs
The site includes recent decisions

FEMINIST LEGAL STUDIES

Feminist Activist Resources on the Net — www.igc.org/women/feminist.html
The site includes material on legal issues

Feminist Jurisprudence Materials — wwwsecure.law.cornell.edu/topics/feminist_jurisprudence.html
Cornell Legal Information Institute's pages give extensive information and links

Women in International Law — www.lib.uchicago.edu/~llou/women.html
Comprehensive listing of resources from Lyonette Louis-Jacques at the D'Angelo Law Library, University of Chicago

Women's Human Rights Resources — www.law-lib.utoronto.ca/diana
Bora Laskin Law Library, University of Toronto

Women's Legal History Biography Project — www.stanford.edu/group/WLHP
Historiography of women as lawyers

Online journals

Duke Journal of Gender Law and Policy — www.law.duke.edu/journals/djglp

Law and Inequality – a Journal of Theory and Practice — www.law.umn.edu/jli/jli.htm

GAY AND LESBIAN RIGHTS

Gay Law Net — www.gaylawnet.com
Australian based site with links to gay laws worldwide

The Knitting Circle www.sbu.ac.uk/~stafflag/law.html
South Bank University's lesbian and gay staff association has a Legal Centre with an eclectic collection of links to resources

Queer Resources Directory www.qrd.org
International links to resources on gay and lesbian issues, including pages on legal issues

Sexuality, Gender and the Law www.lib.uchicago.edu/~llou/sexlaw.html
Comprehensive listing of resources by Lyonette Louis Jacques at D'Angelo Law Library, University of Chicago

Online journal

National Journal of Sexual Orientation Law metalab.unc.edu/gaylaw

IMMIGRATION LAW

See also Constitutional Law above and Human Rights p 60

BCL Immgration Services www.visa-free.com
International immigration and nationality law since 1988

Electronic Immigration Network www.ein.org.uk
The site contains a comprehensive set of links to worldwide resources on immigration law. Access to Immigration Appeal Tribunal determinations is only available to subscribing members

European Centre for Minority Issues www.ecmi.de
Organisation to promote peaceful co-existence between minorities in Europe

European Council on Refugees and Exiles www.ecre.org
Umbrella organisation for cooperation between NGOs in Europe on asylum and refugees. The site includes ELENA: European Legal Network on Asylum, a legal forum for practitioners

Immigration Advisory Service www.vois.org.uk/ias
Free advice and representation in immigration and asylum matters

UK Immigration Sources on the Web www.analyticalq.com/immigration
An eclectic list of links to immigration resources

INTELLECTUAL PROPERTY

See also Information Technology Law

Starting points

Findlaw Intellectual Property page www.findlaw.com/01topics/23intellectprop/index.html
Mainly American resources

Hieros Gamos Guide to Intellectual Property Law www.hg.org/intell.html
Comprehensive site, with links to all jurisdictions

Lex Mercatoria www.jus.uio.no/lm/toc/x.00-intellectual.property.html
Intellectual property pages on this comprehensive site, with links to documents and websites

Researching Intellectual Property Law www.lib.uchicago.edu/~llou/intlip.html
Guide to internet resources by Lyonette Louis-Jacques, D'Angelo Law Library, University of Chicago

Other materials

Advertising Law Resource Center www.lawpublish.com
Mainly American links

ECUP www.eblida.org/ecup
European Copyright User Platform. Information on European copyright developments

IPR Helpdesk www.cordis.lu/ipr-helpdesk/en/home.html
Intellectual Property Rights Helpdesk: A mass of practical information on the European Union's CORDIS pages

SCRIPT www.law.ed.ac.uk/script/pubs.htm
Shepherd & Wedderburn Centre for Research into Intellectual Property and Technology at Edinburgh University. Contains publications and articles as well as links

Oxford Intellectual Property Research Centre www.oiprc.ox.ac.uk
Contains a Working and Seminar Paper Series among other information

Organisations

CIPA: Chartered Institute of Patent Agents	www.cipa.org.uk
Copyright Licensing Agency	www.cla.co.uk
EU Office for Harmonisation in the Internal Market	oami.eu.int
European Patent Office	www.european-patent-office.org
International Federation of Reproduction Rights Organisations	www.ifrro.org
UK Patent Office	www.patent.gov.uk
WIPO: World Intellectual Property Organisation	www.wipo.org

Online journals

Digital Technology Law Journal (Murdoch University)	wwwlaw.murdoch.edu.au/dtlj
Intellectual Property and Technology Forum (Boston College)	infoeagle.bc.edu/bc_org/avp/law/st_org/iptf
Intellectual Property and Technology (University of Pittsburgh)	www.pitt.edu/~stls
Intellectual Property Magazine	www.ipmag.com
Journal of Intellectual Property Law (Georgia University)	www.lawsch.uga.edu/~jipl
Tulane Journal of Technology and Intellectual Property	www.law.tulane.edu/journals/jtip/index.html

ISLAMIC LAW

Centre of Islamic and Middle Eastern Law   www.soas.ac.uk/centres/islamiclaw
Research Centre at the School of Oriental & African Studies, London University

Islamic Legal Studies Newsletter   www.law.harvard.edu/programs/ILSP/spring99
Published by the Islamic Legal Studies Program at Harvard Law School

LEGAL HISTORY

Bracton's De Legibus   bracton.law.cornell.edu/bracton/Common/index.html
In full text from Cornell University

British Legal History   www.lgu.ac.uk/lawlinks/history.htm
Comprehensive page of links and other information from London Guildhall Department of Law

Selden Society   www.selden-society.qmw.ac.uk
The site includes indexes to its prestigious publications

Online journal

Forum historiae iuris   www.rewi.hu-berlin.de/FHI

LEGAL THEORY

Critical legal Theory   wwwsecure.law.cornell.edu/topics/critical_theory.html
Cornell University Legal Information Institute materials

Deborah Charles Publications   www.legaltheory.demon.co.uk
Formerly publishers of several of the leading legal theory journals, the site contains links to selected articles from these, and useful links to other organisations in the field

Jurisprudence
Cornell University Legal Information Institute materials

wwwsecure.law.cornell.edu/topics/jurisprudence.html

Law in Popular Culture
Site at the Tarlton Law Library, University of Texas

tarlton.law.utexas.edu/lpop/lpop.htm

MARITIME LAW

Admiralty Law.com
Site hosted by Giaschi & Margolis, a Canadian law firm, with recent cases and a comprehensive page of maritime law links

www.admiraltylaw.com

Institute of Maritime Law
This site at the University of Southampton contains an impressively comprehensive set of links

www.soton.ac.uk/~iml

Organisations

International Maritime Organisation	www.imo.org
BIMCO – Baltic & International Maritime Council	www.bimco.dk
Chamber of Shipping	www.british-shipping.org
Society of Maritime Arbitrators	www.smany.org

MEDICAL AND MENTAL HEALTH LAW

Starting points

BIOME
Internet resources in health and life sciences. This includes the OMNI gateway and also a BioResearch, gateway covering biomedical research

biome.ac.uk

National Reference Center for Bioethics Literature   www.georgetown.edu/research/nrcbl
Comprehensive site, including Bioethicsline, the US National Library of Medicine links to citations in bioethics literature

OMNI   omni.ac.uk
Organising Medical Networked Information. A gateway to web materials, including a section on Law, Jurisprudence and Medical Ethics

Other materials

Annual Review of Population Law   www.law.harvard.edu/programs/annual_review
Harvard Law School's site contains worldwide material relating to population policies, reproductive health, and women's rights

Bazelon Center for Mental Health Law   www.bazelon.org
Run by an American non-profit legal advocacy organisation for the civil rights of people with mental disability, this site has lots of information

Biomedical and Health Care Ethics Resources   www.ethics.ubc.ca/resources/biomed
Material at the Centre for Applied Ethics, University of British Columbia

BioNews   www.progress.org.uk/news/bionews/index.html
Weekly digest of news in assisted reproduction and human genetics

David Evans   www.davidevans-law.co.uk
A useful site from a health service lawyer mainly dealing with medical negligence in the NHS, and including Health Law Focus, a regularly updated newsletter with new material

Department of Health   www.doh.gov.uk
All the official material on health policies, including many full text documents. The site also includes links to other medical websites

Grateful Med   igm.nlm.nih.gov
The site includes access to Medline, Aidsline, Bioethicsline and other medical databases

HyperGuide to the Mental Health Act　　　　　　www.hyperguide.co.uk/mha
This annotated version of the Act includes a lot of material on mental health law

Lord Chancellor's Department: Individual and Family Matters　　www.open.gov.uk/lcd/family/famfr.htm
This section on the LCD site includes material on Mental Incapacity

Medical Litigation Online　　　　　　　　　　　　www.medneg.com
Medical negligence information service, including a useful index to cases and articles, though you need to subscribe for full text

The Mental Health Act　　　　　　　　　　　　www.mha.inuk.com
A 'walkthrough' the Act and a great deal of other information on mental health

Voluntary Euthanasia Society　　　　　　　　　www.ves.org.uk
The site includes factsheets on various topics, including law, with descriptions of important cases and other legal issues

Online journals

British Medical Journal　　　　　　　　　　　www.bmj.com
Health Information on the Internet　　　www.wellcome.ac.uk/en/1/homlibinfacthii.html
Forensic Psychiatry Online　　　　　　　　www.priory.com/forpsy.htm

MILITARY LAW

Aspals Legal Pages　　　　　ourworld.compuserve.com/homepages/Aspals
The definitive site for military law. It includes summaries of case law, a reading list on military legal issues, information on the courts martial system and international links

International Society for Military Law and the Law of War　　www.alphaway.com/int-soc-mil-law
The site includes a documentation centre and publications

40

Military Law and Justice   www.court-martial.com
Mainly American (non-Department of Defense) but also includes international material

PROPERTY LAW

DETR   www.detr.gov.uk
Department of the Environment, Transport and the Regions

Land Registry   www.landreg.gov.uk
Government agency

Landlord & Tenant News   www.btinternet.com/~david.b.taylor/index.htm
This site includes news, case notes and commentaries

Partywalls.com   www.partywalls.com
Resources on the operation of the Party Walls Act 1996 and its effect on land and property

Property Law for Solicitors and Surveyors   www.garywebber.co.uk
This site includes articles

SOCIAL WELFARE LAW

Department of Social Security   www.dss.gov.uk
Links to the separate agencies, press releases, publications and other information

Ferret Information Systems   www.ferret.co.uk
Advisory services in the field of social security and housing, benefits law and practice

National Association of Citizens Advice Bureaux   www.nacab.org.uk
The site includes information on areas of social policy

Social Security and Child Support Commissioners   www.hywels.demon.co.uk/commrs
The site includes recent Commissioners' Decisions

SOSIG: Social Welfare   www.sosig.ac.uk/social_welfare
Links to resources on the Social Science Information Gateway

OTHER JURISDICTIONS

Gateways

AustLII World Law   www.austlii.edu.au/links/World
Index to countries. You can also browse different materials by country, such as parliaments, legislation, courts, etc

CataLaw   www.catalaw.com/region/Countries.shtml
Legal resources by country and by region

Cornell Legal Information Institute   www.law.cornell.edu/world
Law by source: constitutions, statutes, judicial opinions and related legal material by country

Forint-Law   www.washlaw.edu/forint
Foreign and international law at Washburn University School of Law. The list combines countries, regions and subject, and contains a variety of links for individual jurisdictions

Hieros Gamos: World Government Resources   www.hg.org/govt.html
A list of all the countries in the world

42

Jurweb www.uni-bayreuth.de/students/jurweb/geo/jurweb-index5.html
Legal information on the internet by continent and country. Site at the University of Bayreuth

LAWLINKS www.ukc.ac.uk/library/lawlinks/jurisdictions.htm
Sarah Carter's site at the University of Kent

Nations of the World lcweb2.loc.gov/glin/x-nation.html
Listing on the Library of Congress Guide to Law Online pages

World Legal Systems www.uottawa.ca/world-legal-systems/eng-monde.htm
The University of Ottawa's comparative law project. Valuable in that it allows access by legal system – common law, civil law, customary law, muslim law and mixed systems

EUROPE

As well as the gateways listed above, the following sites provide access to materials on European jurisdictions. See also European Union below p 48

Consolidating European Public Law http://www.iue.it/LAW/conseulaw
A project at the European University Institute. The site includes detailed legal resources for each European Union country and other materials

ELSweb www2.unimaas.nl/~elsweb
The University of Maastricht's guide to European jurisdictions is organised to provide an overview of the legal systems

European Newspapers ajr.newslink.org/nonuse.html
Links to online versions of newspapers by country, on AJR Newslink's pages

Governments On-Line europa.eu.int/abc/governments/index_en.html
The Council of the European Union's links to European governmental websites

Guide to European Legal Databases　　　www.llrx.com/features/europe.htm
Useful guide by Mirela Roznovschi on the LLRX pages

Legal Resources in Europe　　　www.jura.uni-sb.de/english/euro.html
Resources by country on the University of Saarland Law Related Internet Project pages

CENTRAL AND EASTERN EUROPE

For individual countries, see also the lists under Gateways and Europe above

Central and Eastern Europe　　　law.gonzaga.edu/library/ceeurope.htm
Extensive list at Gonzaga University Law Library, with links to individual countries

East European Constitutional Review　　　www.law.nyu.edu/eecr
Online journal from New York University

Guide to European Legal Databases　　　www.llrx.com/features/europe5.htm
Mirela Roznovschi's guide includes detailed information on a number of East European jurisdictions

Other European Countries　　　www.jura.uni-sb.de/english/euro.html#nonMS
Links on the University of Saarland's Legal Resources in Europe pages

Jurweb　　　www.uni-bayreuth.de/students/jurweb/geo/jurweb-index5.html#europa
Links to material by country, including all East European jurisdictions

UNITED STATES

Cornell Legal Information Institute　　　www.law.cornell.edu
This contains (among much else) Supreme Court decisions and the US Code

GPO Gate　　　www.gpo.ucop.edu
A gateway to Federal information on the Government Printing Office's databases, hosted by the University of California. Contains laws, regulations, reports and data for public access

Guide to United States Law lcweb2.loc.gov/glin/us.html
The Library of Congress site

JURIST jurist.law.pitt.edu
The Legal Education Network. Links to a wide range of academically orientated legal resources and legal news

THOMAS thomas.loc.gov
Legislative information on the internet: the Library of Congress's legislative database

CANADA

JURIST Canada jurist.law.utoronto.ca
The Law Professor's network. A clearinghouse for academically authored or otherwise significant Canadian legal resources

Laws of Canada canada.justice.gc.ca/Loireg/index_en.html
The Canadian Department of Justice's website

La Recherche Documentaire en Droit www.bibl.ulaval.ca/ress/droit
Bibliothèque de Droit de l'Université Laval

Revue Juridique Thémis www.droit.umontreal.ca/pub/themis/I
Journal published at the Université de Montréal

LATIN AMERICA AND THE CARIBBEAN

America www.uni-bayreuth.de/students/jurweb/geo/jurweb-index5.html#amerika
Links to material for all American jurisdictions on the Jurweb site

El Derecho Org derecho.org
Includes editions for Latin American countries

Latin America
www.austlii.edu.au/links/2265.html
Links to materials on the AustLII site (Australian Legal Information Institute)

Latin America and the Caribbean
www1.worldbank.org/legal/legla.html
Resources on the World Bank's Law & Justice site

World Legal Materials from South America
www.law.cornell.edu/world/samerica.html
Links to legislation, governments, constitutions and other materials on the Cornell Legal Information Institute pages

MIDDLE EAST AND NORTH AFRICA

Centre of Islamic and Middle Eastern Law
www.soas.ac.uk/Centres/IslamicLaw
School of Oriental and African Studies, University of London

Legal 500: Middle East
www.icclaw.com/lfe/frames/mide_fr.htm
List of the major law firms in the Middle East

Middle East
www.law.ecel.uwa.edu.au/intlaw/middle_east.htm
List of resources on the University of Western Australia's Public International Law site

World Legal Materials from the Middle East
www.law.cornell.edu/world/mideast.html
Material by country on the Cornell Legal Information Institute site

AFRICA

Africa
www.austlii.edu.au/links/250.html
Links to materials on the AustLII site (Australian Legal Information Institute)

Africa
www.uni-bayreuth.de/students/jurweb/geo/jurweb-index5.html#afrika
Links to material by country on the Jurweb site

Bibliothèque des Droits Africains   lafrique.free.fr
Legal materials on African jurisdictions

Law and Development in Africa   www1.worldbank.org/legal/legaf.html
Numerous resources on the World Bank's Law & Justice site

World Legal Material from Africa   www.law.cornell.edu/world/africa.html
Links to legislation, governments, constitutions and other materials on the Cornell Legal Information Institute pages

ASIA

Asia   www.austlii.edu.au/links/249.html
Links to legal resources by region on the Australian Legal Information Institute pages (AustLII). There are links to Asia, North Asia, Central Asia and Southeast Asia

China Online   www.chinaonline.com
This site contains some interesting materials on commercial law

Chinalaw   www.qis.net/chinalaw
Information on Chinese law and the legal system in greater China, at the University of Maryland School of Law

Hong Kong Department of Justice   www.info.gov.hk/justice/laws
The laws of Hong Kong

Hong Kong Judiciary   www.info.gov.hk/jud/eindex.htm
Includes judgments of the Court of Final Appeal

Internet Chinese Legal Research Center   ls.wustl.edu/Chinalaw
Links to Chinese legal resources from the Washington University School of Law Library

Legal 500: Asia Pacific   www.icclaw.com/as500/frames/asia_fr.htm
List of the major law firms in Asia and the Pacific

Project DIAL www.austlii.edu.au/links/2026.html
Developing the Internet for Asian Law. A project supported by the Asian Development Bank and hosted on AustLII's pages

AUSTRALASIA AND THE PACIFIC

AustLII www.law.cornell.edu/world/mideast.html
Australian Legal Information Institute. This site includes Australian Federal and State legislation and case law in full text, fully hyperlinked

JURIST Australia law.anu.edu.au/jurist
A clearinghouse of academically authored and other quality Australian legal resources. A mine of information

New Zealand www.austlii.edu.au/links/242.html
Links to New Zealand resources on the AustLII pages

Pacific Law Materials www.vanuatu.usp.ac.fj/Paclawmat/Paclawmat_MAIN.html
Cases and legislation from countries in the South Pacific region. Site includes the full text of the Journal of South Pacific Law

EUROPEAN UNION

Starting points

Europa europa.eu.int
The European Union's server. Access to all the official EU sites. This site is designed to be all things to all users, so it is sometimes useful to use alternative ways in

Thematic A-Z index to Europa europa.eu.int/comm/atoz_en.htm
Useful if you want to see what is in the Europa site

European Union Internet Resources   www.lib.berkeley.edu/GSSI/eu.html
A rearrangement of the Europa materials from Berkeley University

Euroguide   www.euroguide.org
An easy to use guide to Europa resources from Essex County Library, designed for public use

LAWLINKS   www.ukc.ac.uk/library/lawlinks/european.htm
Sarah Carter's website at the University of Kent

University of Mannheim EDC   www.uni-mannheim.de/users/ddz/edz
Very useful resource for European information

Search engines and databases

COM Documents and Official Journals   www.europarl.eu.int/basicdoc/en/basicdoc.htm
The EUR-Lex index and COM documents index

Euroferret   www.euroferret.com
A search engine for EU web pages

Official Documents   europa.eu.int/comm/off/index_en.htm
This site includes green & white papers, reports, communications, programmes and other resources

RAVE   www.jura.uni-duesseldorf.de/rave/e/englhome.htm
An index to court decisions and articles in journals on public international law and European law. From 1995. Over 180 journals are covered, with links to full text online where available

SCADplus   europa.eu.int/scadplus/scad_en.htm
A searchable database of EU policies and programmes, with a bibliographic resource for tracing journal articles

EUROPEAN UNION INSTITUTIONS

European Union Institutions: comprehensive list	www.europarl.eu.int/institutions/en
Committee of the Regions	www.cor.eu.int
Council of the European Union	ue.eu.int/en/summ.htm
Court of Auditors	europa.eu.int/ca/caudit.html
Directorates General and Agencies	europa.eu.int/comm/dgs_en.htm
Economic and Social Committee	www.esc.eu.int
European Central Bank	www.ecb.int
European Commission	europa.eu.int/comm/index_en.htm
European Court of Justice	europa.eu.int/cj/en/index.htm
European Investment Bank	www.eib.org
European Ombudsman	www.euro-ombudsman.eu.int/home/en
European Parliament	www.europarl.eu.int/sg/tree/en
European University Institute	www.iue.it
Europol	www.europol.eu.int

EUROPEAN LAW

Primary and secondary law

Eur-Lex   europa.eu.int/eur-lex/en
The official database for European Law, including the Official Journal, the Treaties, case law and legislation in force

CELEX   europa.eu.int/celex/htm/celex_en.htm
The official legal database, for which a password is required. This is also available in a number of commercially produced versions, which may be subscribed to in universities or law firms

EU Law and Judgments www.uni-mannheim.de/users/ddz/edz/biblio/opace.html
The University of Mannheim European Documentation Centre site allows searching for full text primary and secondary law, judgments, and other EU documents

Legislative process

Pre-Lex europa.eu.int/prelex/apcnet.cfm?CL=en
Official database for monitoring the decision making process between EU institutions

Legislative Observatory www.europarl.eu.int/r/dors/oeil/en
The European Parliament's site for searching the legislative process of the EU

Unofficial sources

European Union News www.smlawpub.co.uk/online/newslet/eunews/index.cfm
A weekly newsletter from Sweet & Maxwell, with recent ECJ judgments, proposed and adopted EU legislation, case notes, legislation abstracts and articles on European law

Newsletter European Private Law www.jura.uni-freiburg.de/ipr1/staff/msk/newsletter
Newsletter from the Centre for European Private Law, Molengraaff Institute for Private Law, Utrecht

Other European Union servers

CORDIS www.cordis.lu
Community Research & Development Service, including a document library, and information on R & D projects

ECLAS europa.eu.int/eclas
The European Commission Library catalogue, useful for tracing documents

EUDOR
Document delivery service (charged)

www.eudor.com

EUR-OP
The Publications Office of the European Union

eur-op.eu.int/general/en

Eurostat
Statistical Office of the European Union

europa.eu.int/comm/eurostat

IDEA
Electronic directory of the European Union institutions

europa.eu.int/idea/ideaen.html

TED
Tenders Electronic Daily, for details of public procurement opportunities in the EU (formerly published as the Supplement to the Official Journal)

ted.eur-op.eu.int/ojs/html/index2.htm

Current awareness

Background briefings
Short summaries on EU policy matters with links to other resources

www.cec.org.uk/pubs/bbrief

Bulletin of the European Union
The monthly record of EU business

europa.eu.int/abc/doc/off/bull/en/welcome.htm

Eurofocus
News items dealing with everyday events

europa.eu.int/comm/dg10/eurofocus/index_en.html

Euronews
News channel offered throughout Europe

www.euronews.net

The European
Online version of the newspaper

www.the-european.com

European Voice www.european-voice.com
Articles from the weekly publication

POLIS www.polis.net/eu1.html
Comprehensive site for European politics

RAPID europa.eu.int/en/comm/spp/rapid.html
Press releases from the European Commission's Spokesman's Service. Daily update

Special policy areas

Agencies and Bodies europa.eu.int/en/agencies.html
Agencies, Foundations and Centres set up following a decision taken by the European Commission or the Council of the European Union but working entirely as autonomous bodies

CFSP europa.eu.int/comm/external_relations/cfsp/intro
Cooperation in foreign and security policy

EIROnline www.eiro.eurofound.ie
European Industrial Relations Observatory provides up to date information and analysis on industrial relations in the EU

EMU-Net www.euro-emu.co.uk
Comprehensive site on European monetary policy with news and reports

EURO europa.eu.int/euro/html/entry.html
One Currency for Europe: the official EU website

Euro www.euro.gov.uk
The official UK Treasury website

Euro Files   **amue.lf.net**
Information from the Association for the Monetary Union of Europe

Euro Information Service   **www.euro.fee.be**
A comprehensive website of financial and other information on the Euro, from the Fédération des Experts Comptables Européens

Eurydice   **www.eurydice.org**
Information Network on Education in Europe includes a database of all the EU's education programmes

Information Society Technologies   **www.cordis.lu/ist**
Research and technological development within the EU, on the CORDIS site

ISPO   **www.ispo.cec.be**
EU Information Society Project Office. Includes legal and regulatory information

JHA   **ue.eu.int/Jai/default.asp?lang=en**
Cooperation in the fields of justice and home affairs

Network of European Relays   **www.cec.org.uk/relays/relhome.htm**
European Documentation Centres, European Reference Centres and other public sources for European information in the UK

Miscellaneous resources

EuroInternet   **eiop.or.at/euroint**
Information resources related to European integration

Europe   **www.eurunion.org/magazine/index.htm**
Magazine of the European Union published by the EU Delegation to the USA

Scrutinising European Legislation   **www.parliament.the-stationery-office.co.uk/pa/ld/ldselinf.htm**
The House of Lords European Union Committee

European Information Association www.eia.org.uk
Links EU information providers across the world

Archives of research papers and documents

ERPA olymp.wu-wien.ac.at/erpa
European Research Papers Archive

European Integration Online Papers olymp.wu-wien.ac.at/eiop
Recent full text papers

Historical Archives of the EU wwwarc.iue.it
At the European University Institute, Florence

History of European Integration www.let.leidenuniv.nl/history/rtg/res1/index.htm
This site at Leiden University provides extensive links to archive materials

Jean Monnet Working Papers www.law.harvard.edu/programs/JeanMonnet
Published at Harvard University. The site also includes European Integration Current Contents, tables of contents to over 100 journals

INTERNATIONAL LAW

Starting points

ASIL www.asil.org
The American Society of International Law. This site includes a list of information resources in international law and much else, including ASIL Insights: articles on international law issues

ASILEX www.asil.org/asilex.htm
Searchable index to ASIL publications, including International Legal Materials and the American Journal of International Law

Findlaw
www.findlaw.com/01topics/24international
International law page

International Law
www.un.org/law
The United Nations international law page

Law Journal Extra
www.ljextra.com/practice/internat
Site designed for practitioners containing articles on current international law topics from the legal press

LAWLINKS
www.lawlinks.ac.uk/library/lawlinks/international.htm
Sarah Carter's website at the University of Kent

Legal Research on International Law Issues Using the Internet
www.lib.uchicago.edu/~llou/forintlaw.html
A research guide by Lyonette Louis-Jacques of the D'Angelo Library, University of Chicago

LLRX
www.llrx.com/resources4.htm
The Law Library resource Xchange site has a definitive Resource Center on International/Foreign law

Public International Law
www.law.ecel.uwa.edu.au/intlaw
An extensively annotated site at the University of Western Australia, with a particularly useful division into broad topics

UN-I-QUE
www.un.org/Depts/dhl/unique
Searching tool for UN Information from the Dag Hammarskjöld Library

World Bank Law Library
www1.worldbank.org/legal/lawlibrary.html
A wealth of resources on international law, including access to publications, link to the RAVE index for searching journal articles in public international law, and the Law & Justice gateway

World Law
www.austlii.edu.au/links/2500.html
AustLII's index includes pages for international law

56

International courts

International Court of Justice   www.lawschool.cornell.edu/library/cijwww
Includes full text of judgments from 1996 and all documents and information relating to the Court

International Criminal Court   www.un.org/law/icc
Documentation on the new Court

European Court of Justice   europa.eu.int/cj/en
Includes recent judgments in full and Proceedings of the Court (summaries of recent judgments and AG's Opinions)

European Court of Human Rights   www.echr.coe.int
Full text of recent judgments and a complete list of judgments from 1959

Treaties

See also European Union above, Human Rights and Private International Law for other collections of treaties

Fletcher Multilaterals Project   www.fletcher.tufts.edu/multilaterals.html
A major site for treaties

Fundamentals of Treaty Research   www.lib.uchicago.edu/~llou/treaties.html
This guide by Lyonette Louis-Jacques at the D'Angelo Library, University of Chicago, gives links to all the major sources

UN Treaty Index   untreaty.un.org
Until recently a free site, this now requires subscription, and may be available at universities

Globelaw   www.globelaw.com
This site include treaties and conventions on international law and international environmental law

International organisations

International Organization Websites www.uia.org/website.htm
Provides alphabetical, subject and regional lists of organisations

ASEAN: Association of South East Asian Nations	www.asean.or.id
COE: Council of Europe	www.coe.fr
EFTA: European Free Trade Association	www.efta.int
ICC: International Chamber of Commerce	www.iccwbo.org
ILC: International Law Commission	www.un.org/law/ilc
ILO: International Labour Organization	www.ilo.org/public/english
IMF: International Monetary Fund	www.imf.org
IMO: International Maritime Organisation	www.imo.org
NATO: North Atlantic Treaty Organisation	www.nato.int
OAS: Organization of American States	www.oas.org
OECD: Organisation for Economic Cooperation and Development	www.oecd.org
UN: United Nations (and all its agencies)	www.un.org
UN in Brief: Access to UN specialized agencies	www.un.org/Overview/brief.html
World Bank	www.worldbank.org
WHO: World Health Organisation	www.who.int
WIPO: World Intellectual Property Organisation	www.wipo.org/eng
WTO: World Trade Organisation	www.wto.org

Index to journals

RAVE   www.jura.uni-duesseldorf.de/rave/e/englhome.htm
An index to court decisions and articles in journals on Public International Law and European Law. From 1995. Over 180 journals are covered, with links to full text online where available

Online journals

Across Borders – Gonzaga University School of Law	law.gonzaga.edu/borders/borders.html
Berkeley Roundtable on the International Economy	brie.berkeley.edu/~briewww
Duke Journal of Comparative and International Law	www.law.duke.edu/journals/djcil
Emory International Law Review	www.law.emory.edu/EILR/eilrhome.htm
European Journal of International Law	www.ejil.org
Indiana Journal of Global Studies	www.law.indiana.edu/glsj/glsj.html
Law, Social Justice and Global Development	elj.warwick.ac.uk/global/cgi/index.cgi
New England International and Comparative Law Journal	www.nesl.edu/annual
Yale Human Rights and Development Law Journal	diana.law.yale.edu/yhrdlj

Miscellaneous international law

Annual Review of Population Law   www.law.harvard.edu/programs/annual_review
Summaries and excerpts of legislation, constitutions, court decisions and government documents worldwide relating to population policies, reproductive health, women's rights and related topics

Chemical and Biological Warfare Project   www.brad.ac.uk/acad/sbtwc
Joint University of Bradford-SIPRI project to disseminate information on biological/chemical warfare issues

European Center for Space Law edms.esrin.esa.it/ecsl
European Space Agency site

Institute of Air and Space Law www.iasl.mcgill.ca
Site for the legal regulation of international civil aviation and the space applications, located at McGill University, Montréal

International Boundaries Research Unit www-ibru.dur.ac.uk
Research centre at Durham University

Transboundary Freshwater Dispute Database terra.geo.orst.edu/users/tfdd
Includes a database of water related treaties and much more. From the State University of Oregon

HUMAN RIGHTS

Starting points

See also International Law above. For material on UK human rights law, see also Constitutional Law above p 24

Diana International Human Rights Database www.law.uc.edu/Diana
University of Cincinnati site containing a large body of documents in electronic form

Diana Online Human Rights Archive diana.law.yale.edu
Yale Law School site containing documents on human rights topics

European Court of Human Rights www.echr.coe.int
The site includes HUDOC, the database of ECHR judgments, links to the European Convention on Human Rights and information about the court

Index to journals

RAVE   www.jura.uni-duesseldorf.de/rave/e/englhome.htm
An index to court decisions and articles in journals on Public International Law and European Law. From 1995. Over 180 journals are covered, with links to full text online where available

Online journals

Across Borders – Gonzaga University School of Law	law.gonzaga.edu/borders/borders.html
Berkeley Roundtable on the International Economy	brie.berkeley.edu/~briewww
Duke Journal of Comparative and International Law	www.law.duke.edu/journals/djcil
Emory International Law Review	www.law.emory.edu/EILR/eilrhome.htm
European Journal of International Law	www.ejil.org
Indiana Journal of Global Studies	www.law.indiana.edu/glsj/glsj.html
Law, Social Justice and Global Development	elj.warwick.ac.uk/global/cgi/index.cgi
New England International and Comparative Law Journal	www.nesl.edu/annual
Yale Human Rights and Development Law Journal	diana.law.yale.edu/yhrdlj

Miscellaneous international law

Annual Review of Population Law   www.law.harvard.edu/programs/annual_review
Summaries and excerpts of legislation, constitutions, court decisions and government documents worldwide relating to population policies, reproductive health, women's rights and related topics

Chemical and Biological Warfare Project   www.brad.ac.uk/acad/sbtwc
Joint University of Bradford-SIPRI project to disseminate information on biological/chemical warfare issues

European Center for Space Law   **edms.esrin.esa.it/ecsl**
European Space Agency site

Institute of Air and Space Law   **www.iasl.mcgill.ca**
Site for the legal regulation of international civil aviation and the space applications, located at McGill University, Montréal

International Boundaries Research Unit   **www-ibru.dur.ac.uk**
Research centre at Durham University

Transboundary Freshwater Dispute Database   **terra.geo.orst.edu/users/tfdd**
Includes a database of water related treaties and much more. From the State University of Oregon

HUMAN RIGHTS

Starting points

See also International Law above. For material on UK human rights law, see also Constitutional Law above p 24

Diana International Human Rights Database   **www.law.uc.edu/Diana**
University of Cincinnati site containing a large body of documents in electronic form

Diana Online Human Rights Archive   **diana.law.yale.edu**
Yale Law School site containing documents on human rights topics

European Court of Human Rights   **www.echr.coe.int**
The site includes HUDOC, the database of ECHR judgments, links to the European Convention on Human Rights and information about the court

Human and Constitutional Rights — www.hrcr.org
Excellent site from the Human Rights Institute at Columbia Law School. It includes a Hot Topics section with pages on current issues such as Pinochet and the Middle East conflict

Human Rights Library — www1.umn.edu/humanrts
University of Minnesota

Human Rights Internet — www.hri.ca
International NGO documentation centre (has been using the name 'Internet' since 1976!)

Human Rights Watch — www.hrw.org
Campaigns, news, issues, commentary and publications

LAWLINKS — www.ukc.ac.uk/library/lawlinks/human.htm
Sarah Carter's website at the University of Kent

Public International Law — www.law.ecel.uwa.edu.au/intlaw
The University of Western Australia's imaginative site includes links to material on Human Rights (general), specific issues in HR, Indigenous Peoples and Women

Women's Human Rights Resources — www.law-lib.utoronto.ca/diana
Bora Laskin Law Library, University of Toronto

Human rights organisations

Amnesty International — www.amnesty.org
Council of Europe — www.coe.int
European Commission Against Racism and Intolerance — www.ecri.coe.int
European Roma Rights Center — www.errc.org

IGC: The Institute for Global Communications	www.igc.org/igc/gateway/index.html
International Committee of the Red Cross	www.icrc.org
Lawyers Without Borders/Avocats Sans Frontières	www.asf.be
UN High Commission for Human Rights	www.un.org/rights
UN High Commission for Refugees	www.unhcr.ch

Online journals

Human Rights Brief	www.wcl.american.edu/pub/humright/brief
Injustice Studies	wolf.its.ilstu.edu/injustice
Law, Social Justice and Global Development	elj.warwick.ac.uk/global/cgi/index.cgi
Yale Human Rights and Development Law Journal	diana.law.yale.edu/yhrdlj

INTERNATIONAL CRIMINAL LAW AND WAR CRIMES

CICC www.igc.apc.org/icc/index.html
Coalition for an International Criminal Court

International Criminal Court www.un.org/law/icc
The official site for the new Court

International Criminal Court www.lib.uchicago.edu/~llou/icc.html
Resources in print and electronic format by Lyonette Louis-Jacques, D'Angelo Library, University of Chicago

International Criminal Tribunal for the Former Yugoslavia www.un.org/icty/index.html
Legal documents, cases, judgments and other material

Lockerbie Trial Briefing www.law.gla.ac.uk/lockerbie
University of Glasgow's School of Law comprehensive page on the case

Nazi Gold   www.lib.uchicago.edu/~llou/nazigold.html
Resources on Holocaust assets, Swiss banks and World War II dormant accounts from Lyonette Louis-Jacques, D'Angelo Library, University of Chicago

Nuremberg Trials   www.yale.edu/lawweb/avalon/imt/imt.htm
The Avalon Project at Yale Law school

UNICRI   www.uncjin.org
United Nations Interregional Crime and Justice Institute

War Crimes Tribunal Watch   www.wideopen.igc.org/balkans/tribunal.html
Extensive information on the war crimes tribunal, with links to other relevant sites

PRIVATE INTERNATIONAL LAW

See also Arbitration, Electronic Commerce, Maritime Law and other subjects under Special Legal Topics above, p 18

Starting points

International Commercial Law   www.lib.uchicago.edu/~llou/intlarb.html
Resources in print and electronic format from Lyonette Louis-Jacques at the D'Angelo Library, University of Chicago

International Trade Law   www.law.ecel.uwa.edu.au/intlaw/international_trade_law.htm
The University of Western Australia's well organised site

LAWLINKS   www.ukc.ac.uk/library/lawlinks/private.htm
Sarah Carter's website at the University of Kent

Lex Mercatoria   **lexmercatoria.net**
The essential gateway for international trade law from the University of Tromsø this is a well organised and comprehensive site including texts of treaties and conventions, model laws, rules and much other material, with links to other sites

LLRX Guide to International Trade Law Sources on the Internet   **www.llrx.com/features/trade.htm**
Law Library Resource Xchange research guide on ITL compiled by Marci Hoffman

Private International Law   **www.asil.org/resource/pil1.htm**
ASIL Guide to Electronic Resources in International law compiled by David A Levy

Other resources

Baker & McKenzie Publications   **www.bakerinfo.com**
This site links to an extensive collection of full text articles

Bibliography of Trade Related Articles   **www.usitc.gov/lawbib.htm**
From 1979 to date, on the United States International Trade Commission (USITC) site

CLOUT   **www.uncitral.org/english/clout**
Case Laws on UNCITRAL Texts: Abstracts of decisions involving UNCITRAL documents

Competition sites   **www.oecd.org/daf/clp/links.htm**
The OECD has links to competition and antitrust sites worldwide

Hague Conference on Private International Law   **www.hcch.net/e/index.html**
This site includes the Hague Conventions

OECD Documents   **www.oecd.org/freedoc.htm**
The OECD has a large database of free online documents from 1990

T.M.C. Asser Instituut www.asser.nl
This Institute in The Hague has a valuable site for international commercial law materials

Uniform Commercial Code www.law.cornell.edu/ucc/ucc.table.html
Hypertext version of the US UCC

Online journals

CEPMLP Internet Journal	www.dundee.ac.uk/cepmlp/journal/html/home.html
Industry, Trade and Technology Review (USITC)	www.usitc.gov/ittr.htm
International Economic Review (USITC)	www.usitc.gov/ier.htm
Uniform Law Review (UNIDROIT)	www.unidroit.org/english/publications/rev-main.htm

Organisations

Chartered Institute of Arbitrators	www.arbitrators.org
ICC: International Chamber of Commerce	www.iccwbo.org
ICSID: International Centre for the Settlement of Investment Disputes	www.worldbank.org/icsid
UNCITRAL: UN Commission for international Trade Law	www.uncitral.org
UNIDROIT: UN International Institute for the Unification of Private Law	www.unidroit.org
USITC: US International Trade Commission	www.usitc.gov
WTO: World Trade Organisation	www.wto.org

Courts

EFTA Court	www.efta.int/structure/court/efta-crt.cfm
ICC International Court of Arbitration	www.iccwbo.org/index_court.asp

| London Court of International Arbitration | www.lcia-arbitration.com |
| Permanent Court of Arbitration, The Hague | www.lawschool.cornell.edu/library/pca |

THE LEGAL PROFESSION

Starting points

Portal to Legal Resources in the UK and Ireland   www.venables.co.uk

Delia Venables' site is the essential place to look for web based resources for the practising lawyer. Her pages include links to all law firms and barristers' chambers with websites, resources by area of law, resources by UK region and Ireland, commercial subscription services. It is also a good place to check for sites and new developments in web based legal information

Other resources

Infolaw   www.infolaw.co.uk

Information for Lawyers Ltd's gateway to the UK legal internet

International Centre for Commercial Law   www.icclaw.com

The internet arm of Legalease, providing information to the legal profession

LAWLINKS   www.ukc.ac.uk/library/lawlinks/profession.htm

Sarah Carter's website at the University of Kent

Lord Chancellor's Department   www.open.gov.uk/lcd

The LCD regulates the legal profession

UK Lawyers on the web   www.law.cam.ac.uk/urllists/lawyers.htm

List of solicitors and barristers on the web from Cambridge University Law Faculty

Organisations

Bar Pro Bono Unit	www.barprobono.org.uk
BIALL: British & Irish Association of Law Librarians	www.biall.org.uk
General Council of the Bar	www.barcouncil.org.uk
Law Society	www.lawsoc.org.uk
Law Society of Ireland	www.lawsociety.ie
Law Society of Scotland	www.lawscot.org.uk
Legal Action Group	www.lag.org.uk
Society of Computers and Law	www.scl.org

Directories

Bar Directory	www.smlawpub.co.uk/bar/index.cfm
Internet Law Directory	www.lawpage.co.uk
Kime's International Law Directory	www.smlawpub.co.uk/kimes
Legal 500	www.icclaw.com/l500/uk.htm
Legal 500: Europe	www.icclaw.com/lfe/frames/euro_fr.htm
Legal 500: Asia Pacific	www.icclaw.com/as500/frames/asia_fr.htm
Legal 500: Middle East	www.icclaw.com/lfe/frames/mide_fr.htm
Legal 500: USA	www.icclaw.com/us500/frames/usa_fr.htm

Online journals

In Brief	www.inbrief.co.uk
Law Society Gazette	www.lawgazette.co.uk

The Lawyer	www.the-lawyer.co.uk
Legal Week	www.lwk.co.uk
New Law Journal	www.butterworths.co.uk/nlj

LEGAL EDUCATION

See also Student Resources above p 10

Starting points

UK Centre for Legal Education   www.ukcle.ac.uk
Supports teaching, learning and assessment in legal education. Newly launched in 2000, the Centre builds on the work done at the National Centre for Legal Education and the Law Technology Centre, at Warwick University

Other resources

Bar Council Education and Training Department	www.barcouncil.org.uk/et
Law Careers Net	www.lawcareers.net
UK Law Schools and Law Libraries	www.law.warwick.ac.uk/cti/lawschools.html

Organisations

Association of Law Teachers	www.law.warwick.ac.uk/ncle/tlresources/alt.html
BILETA: British & Irish Law Education and Technology Association	www.bileta.ac.uk
SLSA: Socio Legal Studies Association	www.wmin.ac.uk/law/sl9.html

LEGAL PUBLISHING

LEGAL PUBLISHERS (MAINLY UK)

Ashgate	www.ashgate.com
Blackstone Press	www.blackstonepress.co.uk
Blackwell	www.blackwellpublishers.co.uk
Butterworths	www.butterworths.co.uk
Cambridge University Press	www.cup.cam.ac.uk
Cameron May	neon.airtime.co.uk/C-May
Cavendish Publishing	www.cavendishpublishing.com
Context	www.context.co.uk
Croner CCH	www.cch.co.uk
Deborah Charles Publications	www.legaltheory.demon.co.uk
W Green	www.wgreen.co.uk
Hart Publishing	www.hartpub.co.uk
Incorporated Council of Law Reporting	www.lawreports.co.uk
Jordan Publishing	www.jordanpublishing.co.uk
Kluwer Academic Publishers	www.wkap.nl
LLP: Lloyd's of London Press	www.llplimited.com
Longman	www.awl-he.com
Monitor Press	www.monitorpress.co.uk
Oxford University Press	www.oup.co.uk
Palladian Law Publishing	www.palladianlaw.com

Sweet & Maxwell	www.smlawpub.co.uk
The Stationery Office	www.the-stationery-office.co.uk
Tolley	www.butterworths.co.uk:2006

BOOKSELLERS AND REVIEWS

Hammicks www.hammicks.com
Hammicks Legal Bookshops Online has an easy search interface and is the best way to search for bibliographic information on law books

Hieros Gamos www.hg.org/lawlibrary.htm#books
Allows searching for law books via Amazon.com and Barnes & Noble

JURIST Books-On-Law jurist.law.pitt.edu/lawbooks/index.htm
Monthly reviews of new law books, with an index of all reviews since April 1999

LISTS OF PUBLISHERS

The following will enable you to trace publishers worldwide

AcqWeb: Directory of publishers and vendors	www.library.vanderbilt.edu/law/acqs/pubr/law.html
FindLaw: Legal publishers	www.findlaw.com/04publications
Publishers' Catalogues Home Page: by country	www.lights.com/publisher/db/country.html

ELECTRONIC LEGAL JOURNALS

This is a growth area, and any listing will inevitably be incomplete. Some journals are designed solely as online publications, others provide an online version. However, in many cases access to the online text is limited to very recent years, to abstracts or selected articles only. Many online journals are only available to subscribers to the print version, or within a particular educational institution's network

Indexes of journals

Coalition of Online Journals　　www.lawreview.org
Lists law journals by subject indicating whether articles are available in full text or abstracts. Worldwide coverage

Electronic law Journals　　elj.warwick.ac.uk
Comprehensive list of information about UK law journals, both print and electronic

US Law Reviews Online　　lcweb2.loc.gov/glin/us-law-r.html
Library of Congress listing of American law journals available in full text on the web

Full text online journals

These are mainly UK based journals of general legal interest. Other journals (principally American) are listed under topic, or may be traced in the lists above.

E-Law　　www.murdoch.edu.au/elaw
Published at Murdoch University, from 1993

Electronic Journal of Comparative Law　　law.kub.nl/ejcl
Published at Tilburg University, from 1997

European Journal of International Law　　www.ejil.org
Published by Oxford University Press, from 1990

JILT　　elj.warwick.ac.uk/jilt
Journal of Information Law and Technology, from 1996

Law, Social Justice and Global Development　　elj.warwick.ac.uk/global/cgi/index.cgi
Published at Warwick University, from 1999

Law Society Gazette
Current issue and archive of the current year

www.lawgazette.co.uk

The Lawyer
Online version of the legal practitioners' newspaper

www.the-lawyer.co.uk

Mountbatten Journal of Legal Studies
Published at Southampton Institute, from 1997

www.solent.ac.uk/law/silrd.html

New Law Journal
Current week online

www.butterworths.co.uk/nlj

On Line Law Review
Student edited journal published at Southampton Institute

www.solent.ac.uk/law/ollr.html

Student Law Review
Published by Cavendish Publishing, now available on their site

www.cavendishpublishing.com

Web JCLI
Web Journal of Current Legal Issues, published at Newcastle University

webjcli.ncl.ac.uk

SUBSCRIPTION SERVICES

These are the major information providers for legal materials in the UK. Students and staff within universities and colleges may have access to one or more of these, as may lawyers through their firm or chambers. You will normally require a password to access them. These are resources for UK primary law for the most part

Butterworths
For Butterworths Direct services, including All England Direct, Halsbury's Direct and Legislation Direct

www.butterworths.co.uk

Casetrack
www.casetrack.com
For transcripts of cases from 1996 onwards. This database is provided by Smith Bernal, official reporters to the Court of Appeal and High Court

Index to Legal Periodicals and Books
hwwilsonweb.com/ddescriptions/ilp.htm
or www.silverplatter.com/catalog/wilp.htm
Index to over 820 legal periodicals, mainly American but including the major UK academic journals

Justis.com
www.justis.com
For Electronic Law Reports (cases from 1865), Weekly Law Reports and other series of law reports, Statutes and Statutory Instruments

Lawtel
www.lawtel.co.uk
For a daily digest of case law and legislation and other services including an articles index

Lexis-Nexis
www.lexis-nexis.com
For a comprehensive database of UK case law and legislation and numerous other services, and access to American materials

CCH New Law Online
www.cchnewlaw.co.uk
For a daily digest of cases with full text judgments

Sweet & Maxwell
www.smlawpub.co.uk
For Current Legal Information, a family of databases including case and legislation citators, Legal Journals Index and other materials. Look under Online Services

UKOP
www.ukop.co.uk
For bibliographic information on official publications

Westlaw UK
www.westlaw.co.uk
For law reports, legislation and Legal Journals Index as well as access to material from other jurisdictions (notably American)

GENERAL RESOURCES

General information

Useful for widening your research beyond strictly legal materials

BUBL Information Service   **www.bubl.ac.uk**
National information service for the UK higher education community, with listings of web resources by subject

NISS Information Gateway   **www.niss.ac.uk**
Information services to the academic community at all levels. Its site provides access to educational institutions, libraries, reference materials, subject resources in the UK and beyond

RDN   **www.rdn.ac.uk**
The Resource Discovery Network provides access to quality internet resources in groupings of subject portals

SOSIG   **www.sosig.ac.uk**
The Social Science Information Gateway is a resource for finding quality information resources in social science subjects, including law

Search engines

These are best for tracing non-law material. For legal resources they are unreliable, though can be useful if your search is for a specific site. Legal search engines tend to retrieve predominantly American material and should not be relied on for UK sources. There are hundreds of search engines, of which these are the ones I use, Google being my favourite

AltaVista   **www.altavista.com**
Google   **www.google.com**
Lawcrawler   **lawcrawler.findlaw.com**
Yahoo   **www.yahoo.com or www.yahoo.co.uk**

74

Library catalogues

Major academic library catalogues are valuable resources for tracing authoritative bibliographic information on legal publications

British Library Catalogue   opac97.bl.uk
The national library

COPAC   www.copac.ac.uk/copac
Unified catalogue of the largest research libraries in the UK and Ireland

Institute of Advanced Legal Studies Library   library.sas.ac.uk
The legal research institute for London University, with one of the best law collections in the world

Library OPACs in HE   www.niss.ac.uk/lis/opacs.html
Links to libraries of all universities and other higher education colleges in the UK

Email lists

Joining an email list can be a wonderful way of keeping in touch with new developments in your subject, or sharing information with colleagues

Mailbase   www.mailbase.ac.uk
The source for UK email discussion lists serving the academic community. You can search for lists related to legal discussion

Law Lists   www.lib.uchicago.edu/~llou/lawlists/info.html
Lyonette Louis-Jacques' comprehensive list of email discussion lists across the world. It is searchable

TIPS ON USING THE WEB

Bookmarks

Once you have entered a site and find it useful, make sure you bookmark it by clicking the bookmarking button on the toolbar (Bookmark in Netscape, Favorites in Internet Explorer). This will save having to retype the internet address. The next time you want to go to the site, just click on Bookmarks or Favorites and click on the site you want to open. You can organise your bookmarks into folders to help in locating them quickly. That way you can build up your own personal library of links

Internet addresses

These are often referred to as URLs (standing for Uniform Resource Locator). They consist of the domain name and often more to indicate the page. Examples of the most common domains names are:

- www.open.gov.uk (UK government). The domain .gov is used for official government sites only
- www.ukc.ac.uk (University of Kent). The domain .ac is used for academic sites, followed by the country. The United States use .edu for academic sites, and Australia uses .edu.au
- www.cavendishpublishing.com (Cavendish – publisher of this book). Company site
- www.bbc.co.uk (the BBC). Also used for companies, but always indicates the country
- www.un.org (United Nations). Organisation
- www.lawsoc.org.uk (the Law Society). Organisation
- europa.eu.int. Organisation (international)

Knowing this means you can get an idea of what kind of site you are looking at, and hence of the integrity of the material on it. You can see from the list that the usage is fairly loose – .com does not indicate the country of origin, but .co.uk or co.fr does. Organisations may use .com, .co.uk, .org, .org.uk or others, such as .net. The only domain names which are absolutely reserved are .gov (government sites), .ac and .edu (educational institutions).

Internet address names always start with http://, but it is not necessary to type this in with the newer browsers, which will automatically add it. Accordingly the http:// prefix has been omitted in all the URLs listed in this book.

If an address doesn't work

Sometimes, you type in an address and you get an error message. This can be because the URL has changed, or because you mistyped it, or the server is temporarily unobtainable. If this happens, you have several options

- Try again – sometimes it will work again immediately, sometimes you may need to wait
- Try typing the first part of the domain only. For example, it is easy to mistype a URL such as www.parliament.the-stationery-office.co.uk/pa/ld199697/lcjudgmt/ldjudgmt.htm (House of Lords judgments), but if you delete the end of the URL back to the co.uk (www.parliament.the-stationery-office.co.uk/) you will get to the Parliament home page, and you can easily navigate forward from there
- NB: This technique is also useful if you want to find out what kind of site you are looking at
- If you are using an older browser you may need to type http:// at the beginning of the URL
- Sometimes, you find that you get a result by trying the search in a different browser

Downloading and printing

Beware printing documents. Two problems can arise:

- Many web pages, especially legal documents such as Acts of Parliament, are divided into several files. You may need to print each section off separately, or you may find you have printed only the index page, not the whole document
- Sometimes you find a document is very long, and you have inadvertently asked for a print of a large number of pages – disastrous if you have to pay for prints

You can avoid these problems by checking before you print. Netscape has a page preview (under File on the toolbar) which allows you to see what you are printing. You can print selected pages. Or you can download the document (Save As on the File menu) and save it to disk. Or you can copy and paste sections of documents. (N.B. beware of plagiarism if you insert these into your own work).

Some documents are in pdf (portable document format), requiring the use of Adobe Acrobat reader. If you do not have this installed, it will download automatically for you. Pdf documents can be printed and downloaded, but you can't cut and paste from them.

Downloading or copying images

You can copy or download images from the web by clicking on the image with the right mouse button. This will bring up a menu from which you can choose to save the picture in a file, or to copy it (for example, into a Word document). This can be useful for incorporating graphs into an essay, for example, but you must be aware that it is illegal to copy a logo without permission.

Speeding up your research

- It is sometimes useful to have two or more internet sessions at the same time. You can do this either by opening two different browsers (Internet Explorer and Netscape). Or you can open a new window by clicking on File and then New Window. This way, you can access more than one website simultaneously

- Some sites offer 'low graphics' or 'text only' options. This can be useful if you find that pictures or other graphics take a long time to load

- If a site seems to hang up on you, you can sometimes kick start it by clicking Reload (Internet Explorer) or Refresh (Netscape)

- Finding text on a page: Use the 'Find' facility to search for particular words or phrases on a page (under Edit on the Toolbar, or type Ctrl+F)

NOTES

NOTES

CONTENTS

INTRODUCTION	2
GATEWAYS AND PORTALS FOR LAW	3
UK LEGISLATION	4
Primary and Secondary Legislation, Progress of legislation	
UK CASE LAW	6
Sources for cases, indexes and digests to case law	
INDEXES TO JOURNAL ARTICLES	9
CURRENT AWARENESS AND NEWS OF LEGAL AFFAIRS	9
Legal sites, News media	
STUDENT RESOURCES	10
Websites designed for students	
DEVOLVED GOVERNMENTS	11
Scotland, Wales, Northern Ireland	
IRELAND	13
UK GOVERNMENT	14
Government information services, Government departments and agencies	
OFFICIAL PUBLICATIONS	16
Indexes and other sources	
PARLIAMENT	17
Information and debates	
SPECIAL LEGAL TOPICS	18
Administration of justice, Ancient law, Arbitration, Business and finance law, Computer law, Constitutional law, Contract law, Criminal justice, Electronic commerce, Employment law, Environmental law, Family law, Feminist legal studies, Gay and lesbian Rights, Immigration law, Intellectual property, Islamic law, Legal history, Legal theory, Maritime law, Medical and mental health law, Military law, Property law, Social welfare law	
OTHER JURISDICTIONS	43
Europe, Central and Eastern Europe, North America, Latin America and the Caribbean, Middle East and North Africa, Africa, Asia, Australasia and the Pacific	
EUROPEAN UNION	48
European Union institutions, European law, Current awareness, Special policy areas	
INTERNATIONAL LAW	55
International courts, Treaties, International organisations	

HUMAN RIGHTS LAW 61	**LEGAL EDUCATION** 68
Human rights organisations, International criminal law and war crimes	Law schools, law libraries, Organisations
PRIVATE INTERNATIONAL LAW 63	**LEGAL PUBLISHING** 69
International commercial law, Organisations, Courts	Legal publishers, Booksellers, Lists of publishers, Electronic legal journals, Subscription services
THE LEGAL PROFESSION 66	**GENERAL RESOURCES** 74
Organisations, Directories	Search engines, Library catalogues, Email lists
	TIPS ON USING THE WEB 76

INTRODUCTION

There has been an enormous growth in recent years in the amount of legal information available on the web. In the UK, there are official sites providing authoritative texts of legislation and case law as well as a large number of sites offering a range of legal materials of varying quality. It is not always easy, however, to find out which are the best sites or precisely what they contain. And, while there is a considerable amount of primary legal material in the public domain, you will still need to use a library for most retrospective research (even if it is a 'virtual library' of electronic databases). After all, the web was only 'invented' in 1993, and most legal web sites with substantive law start from around 1996 or later.

This book will remove some of the frustrations of doing legal research on the web by indicating the best sites with a description of the contents and scope of each. It concentrates on the UK, the EU and international law but provides you with ways of finding out what is available for other jurisdictions as well. However, the internet is dynamic: websites move their addresses or are sometimes temporarily inaccessible, and new sites with valuable resources are added daily. Some of the information in this book, therefore, will be out of date by the time you read this. But, by becoming familiar with the best sites in the areas you are interested and using the gateways and portals which are indicated under each section of the book, you can keep yourself up to date.

Sarah Carter
University of Kent